Introduction

For sheer indulgence, a bowl of homemade ice cream takes a lot of beating (as does the ice cream itself). For the creamiest results it is important that the ice crystals are broken up as soon as they form. This is easily achieved in a sorbetière or ice cream maker, but you don't need sophisticated equipment to make excellent ice cream - just patience and a firm wrist or hand-held electric mixer.

Use only top quality ingredients and remember to transfer firm ice cream to the refrigerator 30 minutes before serving to allow it to soften and 'ripen'. Alternatively, soften hard ice cream by warming it briefly in a microwave. Never refreeze ice cream after doing this.

Written by Marey Kurz

All spoon
1 tablesp
1 teaspo

Follow Ei
and NEV
not interchangeable.

Eggs used are a medium size 3 unless otherwise stated.

Use unsalted butter for preference.

Freezing times listed in recipes refer to ice creams prepared in a home freezer; if using a freestanding ice cream maker, refer to your handbook for timing.

For additional hints and tips on preparing basic vanilla, chocolate or nut ice cream, and making Hot Raspberry Sauce, Black Forest Sundae or Chocolate Nut Sundae, see step-by-step instructions and pictures on pages 18-19 and 34-35.

Kilojoules and kilocalories at the end of each recipe are represented by the letters kJ and kcal.

This edition published 1995 by Merehurst Limited,
Ferry House, 51-57 Lacy Road, Putney,
London SW15 1PR
Copyright © Gräfe und Unzer GmbH 1992 Munich
ISBN 1 874567 61 1

Honey and Lime Ice Cream

Serves 6-8

Sophisticated ice cream with a hint of honey.

Preparation time: about 20 minutes plus cooling
Freezing time: 7-8 hours

Grated rind and juice of 2 limes, see Tip
4 tablespoons water
60g (2oz/¼ cup) preserving sugar
4 tablespoons pale creamy honey
250ml (8fl oz/1 cup) double (thick) cream

DECORATION
Lime slices
Mint leaves
Small spray of fresh flowers

1 Combine grated lime rind, measured water and preserving sugar in a saucepan. Stir over moderate heat until sugar has dissolved, then bring to the boil without further stirring.

2 When syrup boils, stir in lime juice and honey until dissolved. Boil for 30 seconds, then remove pan from heat. Cover with a clean cloth and set aside for 1 hour to cool and thicken. Unless using a free-standing ice cream maker, turn freezer to coldest setting.

3 Whip cream in a bowl until thick, then carefully fold in cooled honey mixture. Immediately transfer the mixture to a deep 1 litre (1¾ pt/4 cup) polythene freezer container.

4 Freeze mixture for 2 hours or until ice crystals have formed around the edges and mixture has started to solidify. Remove from the freezer and beat ice cream until smooth.

5 Cover ice cream and return to freezer. Repeat the beating process twice more, then leave ice cream until solid. Return freezer to normal setting.

6 Before serving ice cream, soften it in the refrigerator or microwave (see page 3). Serve in scoops on individual plates, decorated with lime slices, mint leaves and fresh flowers.

TIP
When grating any citrus fruit, work over a sheet of greaseproof paper. Use a pastry brush to remove all the rind from the grater, then use the same brush to sweep the rind from the paper into the bowl or saucepan.

Approximate nutritional value per portion:
550kJ/130kcal
Protein: 1g
Fat: 6g
Carbohydrate: 12g

Honey and Lime Ice Cream

Berry Sorbet

Serves 4

The ultimate refreshment for hot summer days.

Preparation time: about 20 minutes plus standing and cooling
Freezing time: 5-6 hours

315g (10oz) prepared berry fruits:
   redcurrants, blackcurrants, raspberries,
   blackberries, blueberries, strawberries
60g (2oz/¼ cup) caster sugar
1-2 tablespoons lemon juice
125ml (4fl oz/½ cup) water
60g (2oz/¼ cup) preserving sugar
Grated rind of ½ lemon
2 teaspoons raspberry brandy or liqueur
   (optional)

DECORATION
Mint sprig
Small spray of fresh redcurrants
Wafers

1 Wash berries if necessary, drain and place in a small bowl. Sprinkle with caster sugar. Drizzle with lemon juice, stir lightly, then cover bowl and set aside for 30 minutes. Stir occasionally.

2 Combine measured water, preserving sugar and lemon rind in a saucepan. Stir over moderate heat until sugar has dissolved, then bring to the boil without further stirring. Boil for 1 minute, then allow to cool for at least 30 minutes.

3 Purée fruit mixture in a blender or food processor, then rub through a sieve placed over a bowl. Add raspberry brandy or liqueur, if using.

4 Unless using a free-standing ice cream maker, turn freezer to coldest setting. Spoon ice cream mixture into a deep 500ml (16fl oz/2 cup) polythene freezer container.

5 Freeze mixture for 2 hours or until ice crystals have formed around the edges and mixture has started to solidify. Remove from the freezer and beat ice cream until perfectly smooth.

6 Cover ice cream and return it to freezer. Repeat the beating process twice more, then leave ice cream until solid. Return freezer to normal setting.

7 Before serving ice cream, soften it in the refrigerator or microwave (see page 3). Serve in scoops or pipe in a large swirl in a glass serving dish. Decorate with redcurrants and serve with wafers.

Approximate nutritional value per portion:
540kJ/130kcal
Protein: 2g
Fat: 2g
Carbohydrate: 30g

Berry Sorbet

Peanut Ice Cream

Serves 6

All the creaminess of peanut butter and chocolate in a frozen taste sensation.

Preparation time: about 15 minutes plus cooling
Freezing time: 5-6 hours

60g (2oz) crunchy peanut butter
60g (2oz) white chocolate
4 tablespoons pale creamy honey
4 tablespoons orange juice
1 tablespoon lemon juice
2 teaspoons orange liqueur or to taste
250ml (8fl oz/1 cup) double (thick) cream

DECORATION
Whipped cream
Chopped peanuts

1 Spoon peanut butter into a heatproof bowl which fits over a saucepan, or into a bowl suitable for the microwave. Break chocolate into squares and add to bowl with honey and orange juice.

2 Stand bowl over a pan of gently simmering water. Stir constantly until ingredients melt to form a smooth sauce. Alternatively, heat mixture in microwave on Full Power for 60-90 seconds, then whisk until smooth.

3 Set melted mixture aside until cool, stirring occasionally, then stir in lemon juice with liqueur.

4 In a separate bowl, whip cream until stiff. Stir 1 tablespoon of the whipped cream into the peanut mixture to lighten it, then carefully fold in the remainder.

5 Unless using a free-standing ice cream maker, turn freezer to coldest setting. Spoon ice cream mixture into a deep 600ml (1pt/2½ cup) polythene freezer container.

6 Freeze mixture for 5-6 hours or until solid. It will not be necessary to beat the ice cream during the freezing process. Return freezer to normal setting.

7 Before serving ice cream, soften it in the refrigerator or microwave (see page 3). Serve in scoops, with whipped cream and chopped peanuts.

NOTE
Peanuts can cause a severe allergic reaction in susceptible individuals. Always advise guests when peanuts are used in a recipe.

Approximate nutritional value per portion:
1400kJ/330kcal
Protein: 5g
Fat: 26g
Carbohydrate: 22g

Peanut Ice Cream

Rum Tortoni

Serves 6

A delicious ice cream based on an Italian meringue mix.

Preparation time: about 25 minutes
Freezing time: 6-7 hours

1 teaspoon powdered gelatine
1 tablespoon water
125ml (4fl oz/½ cup) milk
60g (2oz) unsalted butter, diced
½ teaspoon vanilla essence or 2 teaspoons
   vanilla sugar
3 egg whites
90g (3oz/½ cup) icing sugar, sifted
1 teaspoon lemon juice
125g (4oz) hazelnut biscuits or macaroons,
   crumbed
1 tablespoon white rum or 1 teaspoon rum
   flavouring

1 Sprinkle gelatine over measured water in a small bowl. Leave to soften for 2-3 minutes.

2 Combine milk, butter and vanilla essence or vanilla sugar in a saucepan over gentle heat. Stir until milk is warm and butter has melted, then remove pan from the heat and stir in gelatine until completely dissolved. Allow to cool, whisking mixture occasionally.

3 Beat egg whites in a large mixing bowl until stiff, using a whisk or hand-held electric mixer. Gradually add icing sugar, continuing to beat until meringue is shiny and thick and stands in peaks when whisk or beaters are lifted out of bowl. Add lemon juice and whisk for 30 seconds more.

4 Whisk cooled milk mixture. Gradually fold it into stiffly beaten egg whites.

5 Unless using a free-standing ice cream maker, turn freezer to coldest setting. Spoon ice cream mixture into a deep 1 litre (1¾ pt/4 cup) polythene freezer container.

6 Freeze mixture for 2 hours or until ice crystals have formed around the edges and mixture has started to solidify. Remove from the freezer and beat ice cream until smooth. Fold in biscuit crumbs and rum or rum flavouring.

7 Cover ice cream and return it to freezer. Leave until solid. Return freezer to normal setting.

8 Before serving ice cream, soften it in the refrigerator or microwave (see page 3). Serve in scoops, with cocktail cherries and wafers.

Approximate nutritional value per portion:
1072kJ/257kcal
Protein: 4g
Fat: 13.5g
Carbohydrate: 30g

Rum Tortoni

Yogurt Ice Cream with Berries

Serves 10

White chocolate and whipping cream give this ice cream great taste appeal.

Preparation time: about 30 minutes plus cooling
Freezing time: 7-8 hours

250g (8oz) prepared berry fruits: redcurrants, blackcurrants, blackberries, strawberries, blueberries
60g (2oz/¼ cup) preserving sugar
60ml (2fl oz/¼ cup) water
1 tablespoon lemon juice
315g (10oz) full cream Greek yogurt
110g (3½ oz) white chocolate, broken into squares
250ml (8fl oz/1 cup) double (thick) cream
1 tablespoon icing sugar

1 Cut large strawberries in half or quarters. Set aside a quarter of the fruit for decoration.

2 Place remaining berries in a saucepan with preserving sugar, measured water and lemon juice. Simmer until fruit is soft, then press mixture through a sieve into a bowl. Set aside to cool.

3 Spoon about one third of the yogurt into a heatproof bowl which fits over a saucepan. Add chocolate.

4 Place bowl over hot water, stirring until ingredients melt to form a smooth sauce - this will take about 10 minutes. Whisk in remaining yogurt.

5 In a bowl, whip cream with icing sugar until stiff; carefully fold into yogurt and chocolate mixture.

6 Unless using a free-standing ice cream maker, turn freezer to coldest setting. Spoon ice cream mixture into a deep 1 litre (1¾ pt/4 cup) polythene freezer container.

7 Freeze mixture for 2 hours or until ice crystals have formed around the edges and mixture has started to solidify. Remove from the freezer and beat ice cream until smooth. Swirl in fruit purée mixture to give a marbled effect.

8 Cover ice cream and return to freezer for 5-6 hours or until solid. Return freezer to normal setting.

9 Before serving ice cream, soften it in the refrigerator or microwave (see page 3). Serve in scoops with reserved fruit and dessert biscuits.

Approximate nutritional value per portion:
680kJ/160kcal
Protein: 2g
Fat: 10g
Carbohydrate: 14g

Yogurt Ice Cream with Berries

Nectarine Ice Cream

Serves 4

This delicately flavoured fruit ice cream is at its best when freshly made.

Preparation time: about 20 minutes
Freezing time: 5-6 hours

⅓ vanilla pod
125ml (4fl oz/½ cup) water
60g (2oz/¼ cup) sugar
4 tablespoons pale creamy honey
250 g/8 oz ripe nectarines
2 tablespoons lemon juice
250ml (8fl oz/1 cup) double (thick) cream
Whipped cream and nectarine slices to
  decorate

1 Using a sharp knife, slit vanilla pod lengthwise. Place in a saucepan with measured water and sugar. Heat gently, uncovered, for 5 minutes. Remove vanilla pod, scraping out pith into sugar solution. Add honey and stir until dissolved. Set aside to cool.

2 Place nectarines in a heatproof bowl. Pour over boiling water to cover. Set aside for 1-2 minutes, then drain and rinse under cold water. Cut a cross in the top of each fruit and slip off skins. Chop flesh into large chunks.

3 Purée nectarine chunks with cooled sugar solution and lemon juice in a blender or food processor. Add cream and blend again until thoroughly mixed.

4 Unless using a free-standing ice cream maker, turn freezer to coldest setting. Spoon ice cream mixture into a deep 600ml (1pt/2½ cup) polythene freezer container.

5 Freeze mixture for 2 hours or until ice crystals have formed around the edges and mixture has started to solidify. Remove from the freezer and beat ice cream until smooth.

6 Cover ice cream and return it to freezer. Repeat the beating process twice more, then leave ice cream until solid. Return freezer to normal setting. If using a fast-freeze ice cream maker, freeze mixture for 20 minutes, then transfer to a polythene tub and place in the freezer for 10 minutes.

7 Before serving ice cream, soften it in the refrigerator or microwave (see page 3). Serve in scoops, decorated with whipped cream and nectarine slices.

Approximate nutritional value per portion:
1200kJ/290kcal
Protein: 2g
Fat: 16g
Carbohydrate: 32g

Nectarine Ice Cream

Marble Ice Cream Cake

Serves 12

This delicious ice cream cake can be stored in the freezer for up to a week.

Preparation time: about 40 minutes
Freezing time: 8-9 hours

4 eggs
125 g (4 oz/¾ cup) icing sugar
1 teaspoon vanilla essence or 4 teaspoons vanilla sugar
375 ml (12fl oz/1½ cups) double (thick) cream
110g (3½ oz) plain (dark) chocolate
60 ml (2fl oz/¼ cup) milk

1 Rinse a 1 kg (2lb) loaf tin with cold water, drain and place in freezer until required. Turn freezer to coldest setting.

2 Place 2 of the eggs in a mixing bowl. Sift in half the icing sugar. Add half the vanilla essence or vanilla sugar. Using a hand-held electric mixer whisk the mixture for about 5 minutes until pale and creamy.

3 Whip half the cream with 1 tablespoon of the remaining icing sugar until stiff. Fold into egg mixture lightly but thoroughly, then spread evenly in loaf tin. Cover and freeze for 2 hours.

4 Break chocolate into squares and place in a heatproof bowl which fits over a saucepan, or in a bowl suitable for use in the microwave. Add milk. Stand bowl over a pan of gently simmering water. Stir constantly until chocolate melts into milk. Alternatively, heat mixture in microwave on Full Power for 60 seconds, then whisk until smooth. Cool.

5 In a bowl, whisk remaining eggs with 3 tablespoons of the remaining icing sugar and the remaining vanilla essence or sugar until pale and creamy. Stir in cooled chocolate mixture.

6 Whip remaining cream with rest of icing sugar until stiff. Fold into chocolate mixture lightly but thoroughly, then spread over partially frozen ice cream in tin. Using a fork and a spiral action, whirl both mixtures together. Smooth surface, cover and freeze ice cream cake for a further 6-7 hours, preferably overnight. Return freezer to normal setting.

7 Serve in slices, decorated with cherries, if liked.

Approximate nutritional value per portion:
930kJ/220kcal
Protein: 4g
Fat: 16g
Carbohydrate: 16g

Marble Ice Cream Cake

Step-by-step

VANILLA ICE CREAM AND VARIATIONS
(Serves 8)

1 Fast-freeze ice cream maker method: Beat 125 ml (4fl oz/½ cup) milk with 250ml (8fl oz/1 cup) double (thick) cream, 90g (3oz/scant ⅓ cup) sugar, 1 teaspoon vanilla essence and 2 eggs. Freeze.

2 Freezer method: Beat 3 egg yolks with 3 tablespoons icing sugar and ½ teaspoon vanilla essence until frothy. Whisk 2 egg whites with 1 tablespoon icing sugar until stiff. Whip 250ml (8fl oz/1 cup) double (thick) cream until stiff. Fold all 3 mixtures together.

3 Scrape into freezer tub or sorbetière, cover and freeze for 6-7 hours until solid.

CHOCOLATE ICE CREAM

1 Melt 110 g (3½ oz) chocolate with 3 tablespoons milk. Stir, then cool.

2 Fast-freeze ice cream maker: As Vanilla Ice Cream, stirring in chocolate with eggs.

3 Freezer method: As Vanilla Ice Cream, stirring chocolate into egg yolk mix.

NUT ICE CREAM

1 Roast 60g (2oz) hazelnuts in dry frying pan. Grind when cold.

2 Fast-freeze ice cream maker: As Vanilla Ice Cream, folding in hazelnuts with sugar.

3 Freezer method: As Vanilla Ice Cream, stirring hazelnuts into egg white mix.

2

3

2

3

2

3

Cocochoc Ice Cream

Serves 8

Rich cubes of melt-in-the-mouth ice cream.

Preparation time: about 25 minutes
Freezing time: 12-18 hours

60g (2oz) creamed coconut, broken into
   cubes
60g (2oz) plain (dark) chocolate, broken
   into squares
2 eggs, separated
60g (2oz/⅓ cup) icing sugar, sifted
2 teaspoons orange or almond liqueur

1 Turn freezer to coldest setting.
Combine creamed coconut and
chocolate in a heatproof bowl which fits
over a saucepan.

2 Stand bowl over a pan of gently
simmering water. Stir frequently until
ingredients melt to form a smooth sauce.
Allow chocolate mixture to cool but do not
let it solidify. Stir frequently while cooling.

3 In a bowl, whisk egg whites with 1 tablespoon of the icing sugar until stiff.

4 Place egg yolks in a separate bowl,
add remaining icing sugar and liqueur
and whisk until pale and thick. Stir in chocolate mixture, 1 or 2 tablespoons at a time,
until mixture is smooth, creamy and evenly
coloured.

5 Beat in 2 tablespoons of the stiffly
beaten egg whites to lighten the
mixture, then fold in the rest.

6 Pour mixture into a shallow 23cm (7in)
square freezer container. Cover and
freeze for at least 12 hours or until mixture is
firm enough to slice. Return freezer to
normal setting.

7 Cut ice cream into cubes. Arrange five
cubes on each dessert plate, decorate
with whipped cream and chocolate
caraque and serve.

TIP
To make chocolate caraque, pour melted
chocolate onto a clean ceramic or marble
surface and spread out smoothly with clean
palette knife. Leave until set, then, holding
blade of knife at an acute angle to chocolate, draw it across to shave chocolate into
curls and flakes.

Approximate nutritional value per portion:
502kJ/120kcal
Protein: 3g
Fat: 6g
Carbohydrate: 13g

Cocochoc Ice Cream

Mozart Ice

Serves 8

This symphony of flavours will ensure a special meal ends on a high note.

Preparation time: about 30 minutes
Freezing time: 7-8 hours

110g (3½ oz) chocolate and hazelnut
  spread
2 eggs, beaten
30g (1oz) ground hazelnuts
1 teaspoon lemon juice
1 tablespoon almond liqueur
300ml (10fl oz/1¼ cups) double (thick)
  cream
60g (2oz/⅓ cup) icing sugar
Whipped cream and grated chocolate
  to decorate

1 Spoon chocolate and hazelnut spread into a heatproof bowl which fits over a saucepan. Stand bowl over a pan of gently simmering water and stir constantly until melted. Whisk until smooth.

2 Allow chocolate mixture to cool slightly, then stir in beaten eggs, a little at a time, so that mixture remains smooth.

3 Place ground hazelnuts in a bowl. Stir in lemon juice and liqueur, then stir into chocolate mixture.

4 Whip cream with icing sugar until stiff. Gradually fold in hazelnut mixture.

5 Unless using a free-standing ice cream maker, turn freezer to coldest setting. Spoon ice cream mixture into to a deep 1 litre (1¾ pt/4 cup) polythene freezer container.

6 Freeze mixture for 2 hours or until ice crystals have formed around the edges and mixture has started to solidify. Remove from the freezer and beat until smooth.

7 Cover ice cream and return to freezer until solid. Return freezer to normal setting.

8 Before serving ice cream, soften it in the refrigerator or microwave (see page 3).Serve in scoops, decorated with whipped cream and grated chocolate. Offer dessert biscuits, if liked.

Approximate nutritional value per portion:
1301kJ/314kcal
Protein: 4g
Fat: 25g
Carbohydrate: 18g

22

Mozart Ice

Pineapple Ice Cream

Serves 8

Tiny chunks of fresh pineapple make this ice cream particularly fruity. For the best flavour it should be eaten within a day or two of freezing.

Preparation time: about 20 minutes
Freezing time: about 8 hours

1 fresh pineapple, about 750g (1½ lb)
2 tablespoons lemon juice
100g (3½ oz) white chocolate
60ml (2fl oz/¼ cup) milk
250 ml(8fl oz/1 cup) double (thick) cream
3 tablespoons icing sugar, sifted
Mint leaves and quartered baby pineapples
   to serve

1 Remove leaves from pineapple and cut off peel thickly, removing any eyes. Cut flesh away from the hard core lengthwise, then slice into very thin strips. Cut each strip into tiny chunks.

2 Place pineapple chunks and any juice in a bowl. Pour in lemon juice and stir to coat. Cover and set aside.

3 Break chocolate into squares and place in a heatproof bowl which fits over a saucepan, or into a bowl suitable for use in the microwave. Add milk. Stand bowl over a pan of gently simmering water. Stir constantly until ingredients melt to form a smooth sauce. Alternatively, heat mixture in microwave on Full Power for 60-90 seconds, then whisk until smooth. Cool, stirring.

4 Whip cream with icing sugar until thick. Stir about 2 tablespoons of the cream into the chocolate mixture, then fold in the remainder. Finally, fold in pineapple chunks with juice.

5 Unless using a free-standing ice cream maker, turn freezer to coldest setting. Spoon ice cream mixture into a deep 750ml (1¼ pt/3 cup) polythene freezer container.

6 Freeze mixture for 2 hours or until ice crystals have formed around the edges and mixture has started to solidify. Remove from the freezer and beat until smooth.

7 Cover ice cream and return to freezer. Repeat the beating process twice more, then leave ice cream until solid. Return freezer to normal setting.

8 Before serving ice cream, soften it in the refrigerator or microwave (see page 3). Serve in scoops, decorated with mint sprigs and quartered baby pineapples.

Approximate nutritional value per portion:
420kJ/105kcal
Protein: 2g
Fat: 2g
Carbohydrate: 13g

Pineapple Ice Cream

Quark Ice Cream

Serves 8

This creamy ice cream is best served fresh, and is delicious with hot raspberry sauce.

Preparation time: about 30 minutes
Freezing time: 5-7 hours

3 tablespoons sultanas
2 tablespoons lemon juice
90g (3 oz/½ cup) icing sugar
1 egg
1 tablespoon warm water
½ teaspoon vanilla essence
250 ml (8fl oz/1 cup) double (thick) cream
90g (3oz) low fat Quark

1 Wash sultanas in a small sieve, drain, then pat dry on absorbent kitchen paper. Chop roughly and place in a bowl. Add lemon juice, cover and set aside for 10 minutes to soak.

2 Sift icing sugar into a large mixing bowl. Add egg, measured water and vanilla essence. Mix briefly with a spoon, then beat with a hand-held electric mixer for about 5 minutes until thick and frothy.

3 In a separate bowl, whip double (thick) cream until stiff.

4 Place Quark in a bowl and carefully mix in sultanas with soaking liquid. Beat in 2-3 tablespoons of the icing sugar mixture, then gradually fold in the rest. Finally, fold in the whipped cream.

5 Unless using a free-standing ice cream maker, turn freezer to coldest setting. Spoon ice cream mixture into a deep 1 litre (1¾ pt/4 cup) polythene freezer container.

6 Freeze mixture for 2 hours or until ice crystals have formed around the edges and mixture has started to solidify. Remove from the freezer and beat until smooth.

7 Cover ice cream and return it to freezer. Repeat the beating process twice more, then leave the ice cream until solid. Return freezer to normal setting.

8 Before serving ice cream, soften it in the refrigerator or microwave (see page 3). Serve in scoops on individual dessert plates, with Hot Raspberry Sauce (see page 34) if liked.

Approximate nutritional value per portion:
550kJ/130kcal
Protein: 2g
Fat: 8g
Carbohydrate: 13g

Quark Ice Cream

Ginger Ice Cream

Serves 8

Go for the burn or chill out with this marvellous combination of ginger and ice cream!

Preparation time: about 25 minutes
Freezing time: 6-7 hours

300ml (10fl oz/1¼ cup) double (thick) cream
2 tablespoons brandy
4 eggs, separated
155g (5oz/1 cup) icing sugar
3 tablespoons chopped preserved ginger
1 quantity Bitter Chocolate Sauce (see Step 3, page 34)

1 Whip cream with brandy in a bowl until soft peaks form. In a separate bowl, beat egg whites until stiff, using a whisk or hand-held electric mixer. Gradually add icing sugar, continuing to beat until mixture is shiny and thick and stands in peaks when whisk or beaters are lifted out of bowl.

2 Beat egg yolks in a third bowl until frothy, then fold in stiffly beaten egg whites. Fold in brandy-flavoured whipped cream with metal spoon.

3 Unless using a free-standing ice cream maker, turn freezer to coldest setting. Spoon ice cream mixture into a deep 750ml (1¼ pt/3 cup) polythene freezer container.

4 Freeze mixture for 2 hours or until ice crystals have formed around the edges and mixture has started to solidify. Remove from the freezer and beat ice cream until smooth.

5 Cover ice cream and return it to freezer. When the ice cream is on the verge of freezing, fold in chopped ginger, then return to freezer again until solid. Return freezer to normal setting.

6 Before serving ice cream, soften it in the refrigerator or microwave (see page 3). Spoon a pool of Bitter Chocolate Sauce on 8 dessert plates and centre a scoop of ice cream on top. Serve with wafers.

Approximate nutritional value per portion:
1596kJ/385kcal
Protein: 4g
Fat: 30g
Carbohydrate: 27g

Ginger Ice Cream

Light Fantastic

Serves 4

Creating an ice cream which is low in calories yet tastes terrific is easy when you follow this simple recipe. Serve as soon as possible after freezing.

Preparation time: about 15 minutes
Freezing time: 5-6 hours

2 teaspoons powdered gelatine
2 tablespoons water
125 ml (4fl oz/½ cup) milk
2 tablespoons caster sugar
Vanilla essence to taste
1 teaspoon liquid sweetener
Pinch saffron powder
1 small ripe banana
2 tablespoons lemon juice
125 ml (4fl oz/½ cup) buttermilk
1 egg white

1 Sprinkle gelatine over measured water in a small heatproof bowl. Leave to soften for 2-3 minutes.

2 Combine milk, caster sugar and vanilla essence in a saucepan. Heat gently, stirring until sugar has dissolved. Bring to the boil, then remove from the heat. Whisk in gelatine mixture until completely dissolved, then whisk in liquid sweetener and saffron.

3 Slice banana into a blender or food processor. Add lemon juice, buttermilk and milk mixture. Process until smooth.

4 Whisk egg white in a bowl until stiff. Fold in banana mixture. Unless using a free-standing ice cream maker, turn freezer to coldest setting. Spoon ice cream mixture into a deep 500ml (16fl oz/2 cup) polythene freezer container.

5 Freeze mixture for 2 hours or until ice crystals have formed around the edges and mixture has started to solidify. Remove from the freezer and beat ice cream until smooth.

6 Cover ice cream and return to freezer. Repeat the beating process twice more, then leave the ice cream until solid. Return freezer to normal setting.

7 Before serving ice cream, soften it in the refrigerator or microwave (see page 3). Serve in scoops, decorated with sliced banana, if liked.

Approximate nutritional value per portion:
160kJ/38kcal
Protein: 2g
Fat: 1g
Carbohydrate: 4g

Light Fantastic

Tiramisu Ice Cream

Serves 8

Tiramisu is a famous Italian dessert. It makes a fabulous ice cream.

Preparation time: about 20 minutes
Freezing time: 5-6 hours

250 g (8 oz) mascarpone
2 tablespoons very strong black (espresso)
    coffee
2 eggs
90 g (3 oz/½ cup) icing sugar, sifted
1 tablespoon almond liqueur
Pinch ground cinnamon
10 boudoir biscuits (sponge fingers),
    crumbed
About 1 tablespoon cocoa powder

1 Soften mascarpone by removing it from the refrigerator about 30 minutes before using. Tip into a bowl, add black coffee and beat until smooth.

2 In a mixing bowl, combine eggs, icing sugar, almond liqueur and cinnamon. Using a hand-held electric mixer, beat for about 5 minutes or until mixture is creamy, pale and thick.

3 Add egg mixture and biscuit crumbs to coffee-flavoured mascarpone a little at a time, beating well after each addition.

4 Pour mixture into a shallow polythene freezer container with a capacity of about 1 litre (1¾ pt/4 cups). Cover and freeze for 5-6 hours.

5 Cut frozen ice cream into slices. Lift out with a palette knife or spatula and arrange on individual plates.

6 Sift a little cocoa powder over the top of each slice. Serve with extra boudoir biscuits (sponge fingers) if liked.

TIP

To crush biscuits, place in a strong polythene bag, close the top lightly and place on a board. Press down firmly with a rolling pin or the base of a pan until the biscuits are reduced to crumbs.

Approximate nutritional value per portion:
550kJ/130kcal
Protein: 5g
Fat: 5g
Carbohydrate: 18g

Tiramisu Ice Cream

Step-by-step

HOT RASPBERRY SAUCE

1 Melt 15 g (½ oz) butter in a saucepan. Add 1 tablespoon sugar, then stir in 3 tablespoons orange juice.

2 Add 250g (8oz) fresh or frozen raspberries and 4 teaspoons raspberry liqueur. Bring to the boil, then remove from the heat.

3 Scoop Vanilla Ice Cream (pages 18-19) into 8 dessert glasses, pour sauce over and decorate with whipped cream and mint.

BLACK FOREST SUNDAE

1 Drain 470g (15oz) can cherries. Tip into a bowl; sprinkle with 4 teaspoons cherry brandy.

2 Whip 250ml (8fl oz/1 cup) double (thick) cream with 1 tablespoon icing sugar.

3 Layer cherries, cream and Chocolate Ice Cream (pages 18-19) in 8 sundae glasses. Decorate as shown; serve with wafers.

1

CHOCOLATE NUT SUNDAE

1 Tip 375g (12oz) drained canned mandarin orange segments into a bowl. Drizzle with 4 teaspoons orange liqueur.

2 Scoop Nut Ice Cream (pages 18-19) into 8 bowls. Spoon mandarins over the top.

3 **Bitter Chocolate Sauce:** Melt 60g (2oz) bitter chocolate with 125ml (4fl oz/½ cup) double cream. Stir until smooth. Pour over ice cream. Add whipped cream and biscuits.

1